THE ORPHANAGE

Richard Bergeron

THE ORPHANAGE

An autobiography

TRANSLATED BY PETER MCCAMBRIDGE

Baraka
Books

Montréal

Originally published as L'orphelinat, récit
© 2012 by Del Busso Éditeur
Publié avec l'autorisation de Del Busso Éditeur, Montréal, Québec

Translation Copyright © Baraka Books 2012

Cover by Folio infographie
Book design by Folio infographie
Translated by Peter McCambridge

Legal Deposit, 3rd quarter, 2012
ISBN 978-1-926824-55-0

Bibliothèque et Archives nationales du Québec
Library and Archives Canada

Published by Baraka Books of Montreal.
6977, rue Lacroix
Montréal, Québec H4E 2V4
Telephone: 514 808-8504
info@barakabooks.com
www.barakabooks.com

Printed and bound in Quebec

Baraka Books acknowledges the generous support of its publishing program from the Société de développement des entreprises culturelles du Québec (SODEC) and the Canada Council for the Arts.

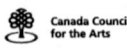

We acknowledge the financial support of the Government of Canada, through the National Translation Program for Book Publishing for our translation activities.

Trade Distribution & Returns
Canada
LitDistCo
1-800-591-6250; ordering@litdistco.ca

United States
Independent Publishers Group
1-800-888-4741 (IPG1);
orders@ipgbook.com

Everything in this book is true…
or false.

Telling the difference
is not what is expected of childhood memories.

Yet childhood does forge
worldview and character,
the foundations upon which an adult is built.

Later, and only then, do childhood memories
really take shape.

Table of Contents

SCARED

I was a big boy.

Soon, I would be four years old. The four of us—the four oldest—were in the back seat of our father's car. The baby was just six months old. He wasn't with us.

A man with a loud voice was sitting up front in the passenger's seat. Who was he? And why was he talking so loud? He had a scary voice.

Later I would find out it was my Uncle Léopold, a really lovely man. The other man, the driver, was my dad.

He looked sad. He smoked one cigarette after another, finding time for only a few words in between. Uncle Léopold answered him at length, in his big, scary voice.

It was night. Night comes early in winter.

Chicoutimi isn't far from Alma, but the ride seemed to take forever. Because everything felt heavy and sad.

We could feel it from the back seat. We didn't dare move, didn't dare open our mouths. But where were we going anyway? They must have told us, the older children, but we didn't understand…

When we got into the car, I think I saw tears in my grandmother's eyes. It had been a long time since I saw anyone looking happy, it had been a long time since the adults around us spoke in anything other than hushed tones, heavy with meaning.

— Not in front of the children, I heard many times.

Even we, the children, hadn't laughed much lately. Something bad must have happened. Something happened and that's why we were in the car.

We drove on and on.

It looked as though we had arrived at last. A huge building began to take shape, bigger than any I had ever seen. And the car stopped in front of what looked like the main entrance.

We got out of the car. My older brother and I each took the hand of a younger brother. We walked up the steps to the main door. The door opened.

Two funny-looking women welcomed us.

Funny, first because of the way they were dressed. They were all in black, from head to toe, with a veil over their heads. Their faces were hemmed in by a piece of white cloth that opened out at the shoulders to become a broad collar.

I would learn later, much later, that this piece of clothing is known as a wimple.

The ladies' foreheads, necks, and hair were all hidden. Did they even have hair?

The whole time we were there, we children—all the children, not just me and my brothers—would wonder if they did. Without ever being able to know for sure, one way or the other.

Funny-looking women, too, because of the way they spoke. Softly, with pretension, with pursed lips, carefully chosen words, and, most of all, looking as though they were overflowing with compassion.

It was definitely the first time I had ever seen women like these.

In fact, they weren't funny at all. Funereal would be a better word.

If I didn't know this word when I was four, I knew what I was feeling all the same. Scared.

Especially since, in this immense entrance hall, the voices of these ladies, weak though they were, resonated as if in a drum.

My father tried to adjust to the way they talked. He spoke quietly too. But there was nothing he could do about his diction and vocabulary: every time he opened his mouth it was clear he was a construction worker, in 1959.

He also kept his head down as he spoke, not daring to look the women in the eye.

Submissive. Humiliated by his lack of education, compliant to what appeared to be figures of authority, my father said no more than a few words.

Uncle Léopold didn't have the same self-control. Uncle Léopold always felt comfortable, no matter what was happening. Uncle Léopold wouldn't stop talking.

Did I tell you about his voice?

Imagine it in a huge hall like that, its walls smooth and hard. It boomed like thunder. It rolled around forever.

Someone must already have told me about hell, without me ever being able to picture it. It was there and then that I discovered it for myself.

I had never been as scared in my life. I think I might well have peed my pants. And I wasn't the only one.

After what seemed like forever, the adults began their goodbyes. Soon it would all be over, I told myself. I didn't understand what had just happened, but at least the whole unpleasant experience would soon be at an end.

My father and Uncle Léopold turned on their heels and walked to the door. Not even a kiss good-bye. Nothing.

It wasn't as though we were expecting one. Back then, such displays of affection were rare. They walked out the door, and closed it behind them. Could someone please tell me what's going on?

The four of us were left standing there, the four children, alone with these unsettling women.

Dad was going to come back any minute, I was sure.

— I am Mother Superior, the shorter of the two said. Welcome to the orphanage.

WETTING
THE BED

Don't ask me what happened next. I have no idea. The chain of events doesn't pick up again until I awoke the next morning.

I woke up in a bed, to the shrill ringing of a bell. Surprise! My bed was in the biggest bedroom you could imagine. One metre to my right, there was another bed. And to my left. The foot of my bed touched the headboard of another. And when I tilted my head back, I could see another bed leaning against mine.

It didn't take me long to work out I had just spent my first night in a dormitory.

Before going on, let me tell you a little about how the orphanage worked.

At the orphanage, you started by learning new words: dormitory, refectory, parlour, the big (play) room, cell (a nun's bedroom), chapel, gymnasium, infirmary.

For now, it's the dormitory we're interested in.

Each dormitory held fifty children. It was divided into two by a passageway that ran down the middle and led to the cells. Twenty-five children on one side, twenty-five on the other. Five rows of five beds on each side. It was enormous!

All the children waking up around me were the same age as I was. Three or four years old. There was nothing strange about that: we were divided up into groups no more than one year apart.

The floor for three- and four-year-olds was just below the floor for five- and six-year-olds, which in turn was just below the floor for seven- and eight-year-olds, which was just below the floor for nine- and ten-year-olds. You will have worked out that the orphanage had five floors including the ground floor.

A few seconds later, I had worked out that the third oldest in my family, a year younger than I, was asleep in the same dormitory. The oldest son, a year older than I, had been sleeping just above us on the floor for five- and six-year-olds. The fourth, barely two years old, had slept on the ground floor, which was where the infants slept.

This system meant I would spend one year with the brother just younger than me and the next year with the brother just older than me. It was the same for the three children in the middle.

At both ends of the spectrum, the oldest and the youngest sons would both spend only every other year with one of their brothers. The result was that, for the longest time, it felt as though I had only two brothers, both part-time: a big brother and a little brother. I would see the two youngest only on vacations, twice a year.

Things were no better for the oldest brother: of his four brothers, he would know only me. And things were even worse for the youngest: a baby when he first came to the orphanage, all his life he would feel like an only child, not the youngest of five.

None of which helped foster a sense of family.

And remember that we were boys, just boys. It's girls who, once they reach adulthood, try their best to make it at least look as though they belonged to a family.

Speaking of girls, there were just as many girls as boys in the orphanage. They were arranged in the same age groups over the same floors, but on the other wing, on the right-hand side of the building.

Which explains why we never saw them. Not even outside: they had their own playground.

Perhaps it would help if I explained that the orphanage was built in the shape of a cross. The left wing—the right arm of Christ on the cross—was the boys' wing. The girls had the left arm.

On the ground floor, the top of the cross was taken up by the entrance hall and parlour. A small chapel used to stand there on the first and second floors, until a bigger one was built, along the length of the cross. The upper floors probably had rooms reserved for the nuns, along with the cells in the middle of the dormitories.

That's probably also where the chaplain lived. He was in charge of sports and the choir.

A good-looking man, the chaplain. A nice man, to boot. All the children loved him, as did all the nuns who lived by his side?

Far be it from me to start any rumours!

Especially since, at four years old, I was completely indifferent to what might be going through the mind of a man spending his life with so many women. Many of whom, no doubt, were rather easy on the eye.

While we're describing how the building was laid out, all that is missing is the main part of the cross. And for good reason: when I entered the orphanage, it had not yet been built.

Now back to the first morning.

I realized I had wet my bed. I was humiliated. Especially since it hadn't happened to me in ages. Every morning, my grandmother, knowing the younger ones had wet their beds, would congratulate me.

No one told me what to do; I followed the others. I got out of bed, trembling with shame and cold.

I saw that some children—around half the dormitory—were busily making their beds. The others left their beds as they were and went to line up at the back of the dormitory.

Which half did I belong to? Was I supposed to make my bed or go stand quietly at the back of the dormitory?

It wouldn't take long for me to get the picture. A nun walked down between the rows of beds until she reached mine:

— So the little new boy has wet his bed! Go stand with the others!

As I got closer, I could see what the thirty-odd children lining up had in common. Their pyjamas were soaked. It was the bed-wetters' line.

It was no surprise to see my brother there. He walked down to stand beside me at the end of the line.

This end of the dormitory, I discovered, is where the toilets and baths were. A tall, stout nun was sitting there on a little bench.

She called the first child over. She pulled down his pyjamas. She grabbed hold of a leather strap and struck him—once, but hard—over his bare buttocks.

Some children shouted and cried, some barely reacted at all. The nun then gave them a cursory wipe with a face cloth. Before sending them on their way with these words:

— If you want it to stop, quit wetting your bed!

For anyone standing at the end of the line and seeing his turn draw closer, it was quite the initiation ceremony!

It was my turn. Then my little brother's turn.

Is there any point discussing the system's educational merits? All I know is that, on my first morning at the orphanage, I experienced the strap first-hand.

Every method works for some, but not for others. I swore I would never be caught out again. And I wasn't.

But, night after night, my little brother wet his bed. Every morning, for six years, he got the strap. And he couldn't have cared less. It was like he was asserting his own free will, telling them "You won't break me that easily!"

It wasn't until much later, thanks to the devotion of Monsieur Bouchard, who, for three long years would get up in the middle of the night to bring him to the bathroom, that my little brother at last stopped wetting his bed.

THE NUNS

How, in so few words, have I managed to be so unfair? Mother Superior bringing the full weight of an eminent member of the pre-Quiet Revolution ruling class crashing down upon my father?

An anonymous nun—who never would have a name—happily beating the children who wet their beds with a strap, day after day? If it all stopped here, you would be left with a dreadful impression of the nuns.

The nuns, just like other women, came in all types. For a young child who would be entirely dependent on them for years to come, only two kinds mattered: the nice ones and the horrible ones.

The neutral ones, the ones we barely noticed even though they made up three-quarters of the total, well, we dealt with them for as long as we had to, then forgot all about them.

A child doesn't analyze. He feels. He feels sensitivity, kindness, goodness, in how people speak to him, how they act around him. He feels the warmth of humanity washing over him. Intuitively, he knows he's not being taken in, that it's all for real.

Fingers ruffling his hair. A hand on his shoulder. A glance. A smile. The sound of a voice. Another step forward when it comes to figuring them out, feeling reassured, encouraged.

And it goes on like this, day after day, week after week, month after month.

These nuns, the nice ones, really did exist.

There were a few of them at the orphanage in Chicoutimi. And a few of them were a wonderful gift. They were enough for a lifetime of gratitude and respect.

Enough for me to say: thank you.

And now, the bad ones. Because there were some horrible ones at the orphanage in Chicoutimi too.

A child needs no one to point them out for him. He feels the brusqueness, the hardness, the bitterness in every word and movement. He tries to steer clear of them.

I've already told you about education by the strap. At the orphanage, the strap wasn't only for bed-wetters. Oh no!

If memory serves me right, it was the primary means of education. For the slightest misdemeanour, the merest trifle, for every time we were late and who knows what else, the sanction was always the same: the strap—although the number of blows varied.

But who had to deliver the punishment? Whose hands held the strap? Somebody had to.

The nun you met earlier, the one who strapped the children when they had just got up, was the one who hit us in the afternoons and evenings, as need be.

She hit us coldly, with no emotion or qualms, measuring out the right amount of force and delivering the right number of blows to fit the crime that had been reported to her and that she had to punish. It was part of her routine.

She went about her work quickly and effectively.

You want names? I won't give them.

Although it's not like I've forgotten. It just goes to show how unfair the world is when I can't remember the names of the nice ones and I can remember every one of the horrible ones.

But what good would it do giving you their names fifty years later?

I realize that, once again, I may have misled you. Because, let's face it, you've started to think the orphanage was some kind of hell on earth. But it wasn't like that at all.

Objectively speaking, the orphanage was organized like a concentration camp. It had around five hundred children and some fifty nuns.

With a ratio of ten to one—fifteen or twenty to one, if we count only the nuns directly responsible for the children—it took rules and discipline. Rules and discipline work rather well, especially backed by the certainty that every misdemeanour will be punished immediately.

And the nuns knew there was nothing better than the strap for nipping temptation in the bud. And ensuring peace and quiet.

All that to say that ruling the orphanage with an iron fist meant the children were as good as gold. So opportunities to punish them were rare enough.

In six years, I was strapped only twice. Once the first morning, then a few more blows years later for reasons I can't remember.

Twice in six years is nothing to write home about.

GOLDEN BOY

It was a basic tenet of survival.

When there were fifty of you to a floor, when you had to change floors every two years, you had to land on the right side of three new nuns every time. You needed to find a way to stand out from the rest. To distinguish yourself. To be someone.

Being the nuns' golden boy was as good as it got.

Who knows how anyone ever becomes the golden boy? At least at the start. Because once you're there, the recipe for staying there comes easily.

You have been at the orphanage for a few months. Nothing has set you apart from the other children yet. Then suddenly one of the nuns sees you reading to another child.

The Three Little Pigs, some story or other about bears or wolves, or *Snow White and the Seven Dwarfs*. One sentence per page. A simple sentence, in big letters.

The nun can't believe it:

— Richard! (With time, she learned my name.) You can read! But how did you learn?

— Dunno. I just can.

— But that's extraordinary! He taught himself to read at four years old. Our little Richard is a genius!

The label stuck. And what a label!

The other time the same nun went on like that was when I made a model of the orphanage.

Those old enough will remember the little red plastic bricks from the pre-Lego days.

On the floor for the three- and four-year-olds, we had thousands and thousands of them in the playroom. With hundreds of little doors and windows. More than enough to build a fair-sized model.

I had been there in my corner playing with these bricks for a good hour. The nun pointed, looked on in surprise, then said:

— Richard, can you tell me what you're building there?

— The orphanage, Mother. I'm building the orphanage.

It was in the shape of a cross, minus the longer part, which didn't exist yet. Everything in proportion.

Count the windows: the exact number of windows in the orphanage. Same for the doors, each in the right place. I must have been on the second or third floor by then.

— But we have an architect on our hands!

We finished it as a group. Ten or fifteen children put the finishing touches to the model.

It was displayed in the parlour for years. To show relatives and visitors how clever and skilful the children in the orphanage were.

An architect!

Here I was presented with a second term of distinction. And a respectable one at that. Architects designed and built palaces. I would be an architect!

From this moment on, throughout my whole childhood, whenever anyone asked what I wanted to be when I grew up, I replied proudly: an architect.

It never failed to surprise, not at a time when the only options seemingly open to the working classes were, in order of notoriety and prestige, to become a priest, doctor, lawyer, or engineer.

— And our Richard is an artist as well! the adults would say.

Who wouldn't have milked it for all it was worth? As it happens, I became an architect at the age of twenty-four.

Only to realize, a few years later, that my real passion lay elsewhere. But not that far away, in fact, in city planning.

Now where were we?

I had been at the orphanage for little more than a couple of months and I'd already been labelled a genius and an architect.

The barrier of anonymity had come tumbling down. I had stood out. Taken on an identity of my own. Not that I had been looking to do that. It had more or less been an accident.

And, accident or otherwise, I understood that what had happened was to my advantage. And that I mustn't lose this advantage.

My findings so far:

- The nuns were more interested in me than the other children.
- They were interested in me because I surprised them at things that were important to them.

- Children didn't matter. It's the adults that had to be won over.
- In the presence of a new adult, the question to ask myself was: What is important in their eyes? What would make them happy?

That's how you become a golden boy. And not only in the eyes of nuns.

For ten years after I left the orphanage, I was able to see that the recipe worked with all adults.

With Monsieur Bouchard, who was impressed by my hard work on the farm.

With Uncle Albert, who was grateful when I got up at five o'clock after a snowstorm to dig his car out.

With Madame Bergeron (no relation), whose every wish was my command. And with how many more?

I can already hear you sniggering at the back: Oh, what a toady he was! Cynics, the lot of you!

Think of it this way: You were born into a normal family, with whom you grew up. You never had cause to be worried, never doubted your status within the household. You always knew that, no matter what you did, you were entitled to your lot.

And so you would delight in exploiting your parents' generosity and patience. All too often, you became egotistical monsters, torturing your poor parents. Nine times out of ten, just for the fun of it, for no good reason at all.

Had I seen you at it, I wouldn't have admired or envied you, not a bit of it. I would have come down on you like a ton of bricks: Idiots! Ungrateful idiots, at that!

At any rate, I would have been in deep trouble if I had ever acted like that.

I had no choice. Like any child, I depended on the adults around me. But none of them were won over ahead of time; I always had to think about how to bring them round to my side. As they appeared in my life, one by one.

Draw whatever conclusions you like! Six years being the nuns' pet. Six years of surprising them, of always giving them more than they asked for.

Evening classes at five years old to hone this precociousness:

— You can count on me, no matter what.

Doing the reading at Christmas mass in Chicou-timi cathedral?

— No problem. As long as I have something to stand on to see over the lectern.

Getting 100% in every subject?

— I won't let you down.

And what else? As long as it reinforced my status as a child prodigy, no expectation was too high, no mountain too steep.

Time for a little perspective. Before you think I have a big head.

At three years old, my son knew all his fairy tales by heart. You should have heard him doing *Bluebeard*:

— You betrayed me, traitor! You shall pay!

When she was four, my daughter could read perfectly. Better yet, she had learned to read *La Presse* and *Le Devoir* at the same time as I did, every morning, from her seat on the other side of the table.

She set me straight. When I let her have it about a bad mark, reminding her what a child prodigy she had been, she retorted:

— Stop going on about me reading when I was four, just like you. At L'École internationale de

Montréal everybody could read when they were four. Some of them in languages as different as Chinese, English, and French!

The worst part is that, having met some of my daughter's friends, I'm pretty sure she was right.

Which sample is skewed? Were standards too low at the orphanage or too high at my daughter's school?

It doesn't matter. Now in my mid-fifties, I've had plenty of opportunities to put things in perspective. I have met many brilliant people—brilliant in all kinds of ways—throughout my life. But the fact remains that, thanks to my cleverness, or at least that which the nuns believed was mine, I was able to become their golden boy. And being the nuns' pet makes six years in an orphanage a lot more bearable.

When I think back on it, I wonder how the other forty-nine kids coped.

Because even for the one who managed to attract attention, to arouse some sympathy, his or her childhood wasn't anything to boast about. It must have been really something else for the others!

They are all my age now. I often think of them, and what has become of them. I hope they pulled through.

ROUTINE

All concentration-camp systems are alike: daily life is dull and repetitive.

There's no point returning to the unbending rule that all misdemeanours would be punished. Because the unbending nature of that rule meant misdemeanours were rare.

And when they did happen, they were caused by a careless mistake, never the result of a revolt or a challenge to authority.

So much so that life at the orphanage was perfectly calm, although a bit dull and repetitive nonetheless.

I have already told you what happened in the morning, once the wake-up bell had been rung. Some made their beds, others lined up for the strap. Routine.

Then it was time for breakfast.

Porridge, always porridge, nothing but porridge. With a slice of white toast thinly spread with commercial jam bought by the twenty- or fifty-litre barrel load.

Then a group of children would wash, dry, and put away the dishes, while another group wiped down the tables and swept the refectory.

There were no dishwashers in those days. And even if there had been, the orphanage wouldn't have had one anyway. No doubt due to belt-tightening. Which meant they didn't have the means to employ staff either.

Chores were up to us children. Every meal. Three times a day. Washing the dishes and cleaning the refectory. Always.

Routine.

The orphanage was a school, too.

From junior kindergarten to fifth or sixth grade. We didn't have far to go: the classrooms for each year were on the same floor as the dormitories.

I was made a classroom assistant. I helped the children who were struggling. I read to them. I supervised them when they were doing their homework. I even corrected and marked their tests.

I never had much to learn at school. Not at elementary school, at any rate.

Because I had taught myself to read at four. And because, from the same age, I was given special lessons on all kinds of subjects. The nuns wanted to know how bright I was, I suppose.

And that's what going to school at the orphanage was like for me. It all made me feel that I was appreciated. At a time and a place where being worth something was vital for me.

School in the mornings and afternoons. Homework in the evenings. With meals in between. Routine.

Speaking of meals, lunch and supper deserve special mention.

Because the food was terrible, as you might imagine. The meat especially. Always in shapeless stews and fricassees. All cooked in enormous pots and pans.

No doubt local slaughterhouses gave the orphanage carcasses of so-called "reform" cattle for a few dollars. You know the ones: the old dairy cows that reach the end of the line once they hit twelve or fifteen. That go into cat and dog food nowadays. It was a far cry from your milk-fed veal!

The rule at the orphanage was straightforward: you weren't allowed to leave anything at all on your plate.

What were we to do with bits of rubber we'd been munching on for minutes at a time and couldn't bring ourselves to swallow? I would suck them dry of every last drop of juice, put them in my pocket, and throw them down the toilet after the meal.

Over six years I must have added a fair few pounds of meat to the Chicoutimi sewers!

The routine also had us go out and get some fresh air in the yard. Once, twice, three times a day, depending on the weather.

I don't remember there being any organized or team sports. It seems to me that "playing" was the only activity on the program. I wasn't much interested anyway.

I kept to myself at the back of the yard, up by the fence separating the orphanage from the surrounding homes. Discreetly, almost unnoticed, I would take a look at what was going on in the houses and backyards.

Sometimes the people who lived there would see me watching and say a few words, always kind. I would mumble something back, embarrassed, and hurry back to the other children.

Malicious gossip had it that I was spying on them. Watching normal people go about their lives was interesting, all the same...

Prayer was a big part of life in the orphanage. Which should come as no surprise, considering it was officially known as the Orphélinat de l'Immaculée (Orphanage of the Immaculate Conception) and was run by the Little Franciscans of Mary.

Everything was a reason to pray. Meals, the beginning of class, going to bed, everything we did, all day, every day.

On top of that were all the events requiring immediate divine intervention.

Advent in the run-up to Christmas was the worst. That and Lent, the forty days before Easter.

Throughout these holy periods, we had to go to the chapel for vespers every day. Not to mention mass on Saturdays *and* Sundays.

From the above, you might think I saw all this religion in a negative light, that it was nothing but a succession of unpleasant obligations. Not at all. Because everything about the orphanage encouraged us to believe very strongly in Jesus. (Would you be surprised to learn that I was a believer?) And because it was just one aspect, among many others, of our daily routine at the orphanage.

It was either that or something else...

One of the things that bothered all the children in the orphanage was where we went after the fifth floor when we were older than eleven or twelve.

We Bergerons were less worried than the others because we had a family. Although...

Some said, without any of us really being able to know for sure, that we headed for "reform school" after the orphanage.

We knew what reform school was because the nuns would bring it up sometimes whenever they were mad:

— Why you little rascal! You're going to end up in reform school. That's where they lock up children who do not listen. You'll behave yourself at reform school when a hooligan in the making takes you into a corner to rough you up!

Quite the program!

Personally, I watched the years going by and saw myself getting older with growing concern. Was I going to end up in reform school in the not-too-distant future?

Thankfully, as it happens, my concerns were wide of the mark: I left the orphanage when I was nine.

Although, come to think of it, what happened right after that wasn't any better than reform school. But let's not get ahead of ourselves. We'll cross that bridge when we come to it.

The question continued to hang over us: Were children who had passed through the orphanage really sent to reform school?

It sounded awful. And if they were sent somewhere else, what became of them?

Since I was destined for life as an architect—well, the nuns had decided for me; I didn't have much to do with it—I felt compelled to observe how the new wing of the orphanage (the main part of the cross) was being built.

It took a long time: two years, I'd say. Because once they put the structure up, they then had to demolish the charred remains after the fire. And build it all again.

I would spend hours, sitting by the window, watching the construction site grow. Even to this day I still obsess a little every time I see a construction site.

Decades later, my children would scold me:

— Come on, Guillaume or Nadianie, I'd say (ten years apart). I'll put you in your seat and we'll go for a ride.

— No way! You'll only drag us round construction sites for hours!

The Saturday night movie was the high point of the week for all the children at the orphanage. It was most certainly in the left wing belonging to the boys. Because I am not at all sure there was also a Saturday night movie in the girls' wing.

One of the two TV channels at the time in the Saguenay–Lac-Saint-Jean region showed a children's movie early on Saturday evenings.

The television was hung from the angle of the wall in the playroom, at least seven feet off the ground. The screen can't have been more than twenty inches. Black and white, obviously. With a picture that left a lot to be desired by today's standards.

The fifty children would sit in a semicircle on the floor. Since the television was so high up, you had to tilt your head back to watch it.

Despite these conditions, the Saturday night movie was quite the party.

There were more or less two types of movies that everyone loved. There were comedies—real comedies—starring Laurel and Hardy or Abbott and Costello, and less funny movies with Charlie Chaplin that we enjoyed all the same.

Then there were horror movies.

Great big rubber monsters like Godzilla wrecking everything in their path. Disgusting characters like Frankenstein lurking behind the door you were about to open.

Or the earth had been destroyed by cosmic ray, nuclear holocaust, or alien attack.

As far as I can remember, this was the only time when the fifty children got to let go, laugh their heads off, and shout in terror without fear of being reprimanded by the nuns.

And sometimes the Saturday night movie took an altogether different turn.

I spoke earlier about my concern at seeing myself grow older.

One Saturday night the movie was about a group of teenagers. And according to the movie, there was nothing fun about being a teen.

The main character, after one prank too many, wound up at the police station. Then he and his gang ran across what looked like the foundations of a new building on a construction site.

— Will I have to do that too when I get to his age? I thought. I'd be scared of falling!

In the last scene, the hero gets behind the wheel of a car and, accelerator down to the floor, races toward a precipice.

The idea being to fling himself from the car at the last possible second. Our hero won—because the guy he was racing against drove over the edge and was killed.

— Will I have to do that too? I'm sure if anyone has to die, it's going to be me!

The movie stayed with me for years.

Later I found out it was called *Rebel Without a Cause*, starring James Dean. An excellent movie, a cinematic masterpiece.

But that's beside the point. Was it an error of judgment on the nuns' part to let us watch it? Or did I just overreact?

Life at the orphanage went by just like that. Humdrum, quiet, monotonous. With something unexpected cropping up now and again.

I would be remiss to end my discussion of everyday life at the orphanage without mentioning one such event, a truly exceptional event.

I'll start by confessing to a little white lie earlier, when I said that nobody at the orphanage harboured any ideas of revolt. There was one boy who always did the opposite of what he should have done... and who got the strap almost every day.

That not being enough, the nuns had to come up with other sanctions.

One day the whole orphanage went on an outing to the zoo in Quebec City.

The whole orphanage, that is, except the boy in question, who was locked in.

Not to be outdone, he ingeniously found a way out of the room. And his ingenuity didn't stop there. Because then he came up with the perfect way to exact his revenge.

Long bathroom sinks, each with a dozen or so faucets, ran along one of the walls in each dormitory. We brushed our teeth there before going to bed.

And what did our little bright spark decide to do but plug the sinks and turn all the taps on full blast.

Since the orphanage was empty, he was free to repeat the prank in all the dormitories. On the boys' side as well as the girls'.

We got back from Quebec City to find the orphanage flooded. Three inches of water everywhere. Water cascading down the stairwells. The nuns got out as many sheets as they could find. And every child helped wring them out. Long into the night.

The same boy was rumoured to have set fire to the new wing as it was being built.

What a blaze!

Back then wooden posts propped up new buildings until the concrete had set. The new wing had five floors, each supported by a veritable forest of wooden posts. The flames were so intense that everyone thought the whole orphanage was going to go up in smoke.

The nuns had us down on our knees, praying for God to change the direction the wind was blowing, or something like that. Five hundred children on their knees, little hands joined together, little eyes closed, repeating Hail Mary after Hail Mary in unison, with all the conviction their little hearts could muster.

God couldn't help but be moved.

In other words, the spirit of revolt was alive and kicking in the orphanage.

But as I remember, real revolt was limited to this single boy.

And don't go drawing any hasty conclusions from the above. For a child, normal is whatever he knows. Which is just as well, since it means a child who spends his summers playing in the lanes is no less happy than the little rich kid at a cottage by the lake. Quebec comedian Yvon Deschamps dispels any doubts on this count in his monologue *Dans ma cour*. Read it and you'll see what I mean.

Personally, I have never seen children laugh more or seem happier to be alive than the kids of Bissau, Port-au-Prince, and Ouagadougou. The orphanage in Chicoutimi was a haven of riches and comfort in comparison.

At a push, I'd even go so far as to say we enjoyed it there.

VACATION TIME

— You're lucky, you Bergerons, to have your family.

That's what the nuns would tell us. Adding that the other children had no one worrying about them outside the orphanage walls.

But if you still had family, what were you doing in the orphanage, I hear you ask. That's a good question. Here's the answer.

My mother and father married in 1952. He was twenty, she was twenty-one. Back then there was no such thing as contraception. Even if there had been, the priests—who still held sway—were imploring French Canadians to have babies, as many babies as possible.

To fill the heavens with pure souls or to overturn the Battle of the Plains of Abraham? Probably both.

At any rate, my parents had five children in just short of four and a half years. They were on pace for ten or twelve. But it stopped with the fifth.

A problem during childbirth left my mother in a coma for months, then paralyzed for life.

Faced with such a catastrophe, what could my father do? A crane operator, he always worked far from home: the Chalk River Nuclear Laboratories in Ontario, then the dam at Chute-des-Passes at the head of Rivière Péribonka, then the dams on Rivière Manicouagan.

Before coming to any decision, it was agreed we should wait until Maman came out of her coma. We waited for three months, during which time our grandmother—my father's mother—looked after us.

There were ten of us living in her tiny apartment. As well as living on top of each other, circumstances didn't help lighten the atmosphere any.

It was only when Maman woke up that we were able to gauge the true horror of the situation.

The right side of her body was paralyzed. Hemiplegia, they call it. The left side of her brain had also been unplugged, to put it simply.

For the rest of her life, she would have the mental age of a child of five, the doctors said. She would never speak or walk again, they said. She would have to spend the rest of her days in an institution. Which she did.

But she did learn to speak and walk again—in every which way, mind you. But it was always something to laugh about. And a five-year-old laughs a lot.

Maman was a happy child for the rest of her life. A happy child who laughed a lot and made others laugh too.

Even today, at eighty years young, the twelfth floor of the Angelica Residence in Montréal-Nord delights in her constant good humour.

My father's world fell apart.

Barely twenty-six, he suddenly found himself without a wife and with five young children to look after. Offers flooded in from both sides of the family to take care of such and such a child and raise them as their own.

— They want to take them away from me —never!

The orphanage seemed like a much better solution to him:

— That way at least, my children will be together. I'll be able to bring them home twice a year, at Christmas and over the summer. And it will only be for a while. I'll take them back as soon as I can.

So today our vacation begins. The nuns told us:

— Tomorrow your father will come for you. You are going on vacation.

In the summer, I would sit on the old balcony at the end of the floor until I saw my father's pale blue car turning into the drive. I would sit there from the early morning, until two or three in the afternoon if I had to.

I would do the same in the winter, this time by the window. Allowing me to withdraw from everyday life in the orphanage to keep my eyes peeled for my father was another favour afforded me by my special status.

As soon as the car came into sight, my headlong race to the main entrance on the ground floor began. Just let those nuns try to stop me!

But they didn't even think to slow me down. Instead, they shouted after me:

— Enjoy your vacation!

— Goodbye!

The car ride from Chicoutimi to Alma was almost too much.

Five overexcited children shouting, laughing, and squabbling for all they were worth. With no fear of us being told off since Papa was just as happy as we were.

And arriving at our grandmother's house was really something! So much so that it went down in family history. My brothers acted just as you might expect. They were happy, of course. Excited, too. But within reason.

I would completely lose it.

As soon as I saw my grandmother, I would start shouting, crying, rolling around on the floor, beating the walls.

My father would grab hold of me to stop me hurting myself. It would last for an hour, two hours, three hours. Until, my energy spent, I was exhausted.

When I finally recovered, I would be on the living room sofa, opposite my grandmother's hide-a-bed. Where I would sleep for ten or twelve hours.

When I woke up, either in the middle of the night or the next morning, I would see my grandmother sleeping just a metre or two away. And I was happy.

Then the countdown would begin. Seven or eight days for the Christmas vacation, double that for summer.

An outrageous number of visitors would come to my grandmother's house, especially over the Christmas vacation. She had had eleven children, most of them married with offspring of their own.

In a rented summer cottage by a lake, my father would welcome just as many visitors, but more spread out, in smaller doses.

Everything would change halfway through the vacation.

Until then it seemed like it would never end. Then everything seemed to be rushing by. And fear would set in: we would have to go back to the orphanage in so many days.

I had gotten into such a routine that I would act just like I did back at the orphanage. I had no interest in the other children. Not my cousins. Not the other boys, let alone the girls. Not even my brothers.

I spent my time with the adults. I would sit at the table with the men and, without saying a word, without making the slightest sound, would watch them play bridge for hours.

Or I would slip into the living room and listen to the women gossip. Often, when the evenings dragged on into the wee small hours, I would fall asleep right there.

They would find me asleep on the kitchen floor, my head resting between the wall and the dryer. Or in the living room, my body curled around the foot of the lamp.

Then they would pick me up and lay me down on the living room sofa that practically belonged to me by then. It was there that I would wake up the next morning, opposite my grandmother's hide-a-bed.

As the days went by, once we passed the halfway point, we grew increasingly worried. Then, without fail, it would be time to go back.

I would direct operations. All five of us would twist our father's arm to at least delay the inevitable.

— After supper, Papa! After supper!

I would even come up with ways to put it off until the next day.

Like the time we buried the car in the snow— only for our father to free it with one heavy foot on the gas.

Things were always quiet on the way back. And sad. Especially since it would be late at night. Proof at least that some of my strategies had paid off.

We would also bring an unbelievable amount of gifts back with us. Our father had spoiled us; our aunts and uncles had not wanted to be outdone.

We often needed two cars to get back. At the orphanage, all the gifts instantly belonged to everyone. My father couldn't get over it.

But I'm pretty sure I've always understood there was no other way. I was always proud that it was my family that periodically renewed the toys for practically the whole orphanage.

As soon as we went back, I returned to being the thoughtful, level-headed child the nuns liked so much.

— Are you glad to be back, Richard?

— Oh yes, Mother. Very glad!

HAPPINESS

Anyone who wakes to a bell or an alarm clock day after day, always at the same time, will know that you come to anticipate it, waking up by yourself a few minutes before it rings.

What should you do with these minutes? Why not play a little game?

When I woke, I didn't open my eyes. I listened and used my other senses to work out where I was. Hearing, first of all.

With fifty children to a dormitory, there was no shortage of sounds. The box springs were no more than metal bars attached to springs on the bed frames. The slightest movement from any one child and the whole dormitory was treated to a noisy symphony.

So close to wake-up time, all the children would move about. The creaking sound they made gave me my bearings in no time. No luck! I'd woken up again at the orphanage.

This particular morning, I let the seconds tick by. No familiar sounds.

But before getting too excited, let's move on to the second test: the sniff test.

A good half of the fifty children wet their beds. With the odd tear here and there, the plastic mattress covers were far from watertight. Especially with plastic in the early 1960s not being what it is today.

Which meant the mattresses were soaked with urine. Not to mention the covers. In other words, a dormitory with fifty young boys sleeping in it stinks.

Was that the case this morning? Surprise! Not the slightest whiff of anything unpleasant.

On the face of it, the sound and smell tests indicated that I probably hadn't woken up at the orphanage. But hasty conclusions are risky: they can set you up for a fall.

Eyes still closed, I moved on to the final test: what could I remember?

Did I remember leaving the orphanage? Did my father come pick us up? Did we laugh until we could laugh no more all the way home? Did we pull up in front of our grandmother's house? Did I roll around on the floor, laughing, crying, shouting like an epileptic? Did we go to bed exhausted? Was I, as usual, allowed to sleep on the living room sofa beside my grandmother's hide-a-bed?

Usually I had no trouble remembering it all.

Usually I had no trouble working out that I was lying in bed at my grandmother's. And then I could at last open my eyes.

But not this time. Try as I might, I couldn't remember a thing. Had I ever forgotten leaving the orphanage before?

Come on—not on your life! So how could I have been at my grandmother's? It was impossible!

And yet for the minute or so my little game had worked, I had still come across none of the usual signs that I had woken up at the orphanage.

Could it be I would be waking up at my grandmother's, even though I had no idea how I had gotten there? Had I been too quick in writing it off as impossible? Perhaps it was possible after all.

My bed at the orphanage had no headboard. And yet I could feel the back of a sofa to my right.

The blankets were not from the orphanage. The slump underneath my butt felt very much like the gap between two cushions on a sofa.

It was time to face the facts. All that remained was to open my eyes and see for myself that I really was at my grandmother's. But what if it wasn't true?

No, it didn't make any sense. I *was* at my grandmother's. I had to be!

That morning, when I finally relented and opened my eyes, I saw my grandmother sleeping peacefully on the other side of the living room. And I quietly began to cry.

With happiness.

Today I am fifty-six. Life has given me its fair share of great moments.

If I had to choose the best of all, it would be that one.

THE ACCIDENT

I was seven years old.

I had been at the orphanage for a long time, so I had had plenty of time to settle in. And become the nuns' golden boy.

But sometimes being the golden boy can work against you.

There were fifty of us per dormitory. A good half of us wet our beds, night after night. The mattresses were soaked with urine and stank to high heaven. But I've already told you that.

The nuns decided to do something about the stench we had to sleep in. But the solution they came up with was foolhardy to say the least.

Judge for yourselves.

They decided to fight fire with fire, or stink with stink, as it were.

They boiled some sort of brew in a huge cooking pot. We could hear the bubbles breaking ominously on the surface.

Pop! Pop! Pop!

The sound was enough to strike fear into our hearts. And we shuddered when we saw brownish fumes rising off the mixture. Not to mention that it really stank!

They must have been boiling the intestines of the devil himself.

People tend to be even more frightened of what they cannot see.

And we couldn't see into the pot. Because it was too big. Because it was resting on a little portable electric stove with two burners. Because the stove itself was on top of a vanity.

You know the kind, the little pine vanities you can still find in second-hand stores today. The vanities that people back then sat in front of to get dressed in their rooms.

A towel rack, a shelf for a basin of water, a drawer, a tiny door right at the bottom, with some storage space behind it.

The vanity, the two-burner stove, the huge pot, all on top of each other—how could a child ever have known what was bubbling away in there?

The vanity sat in the middle of the dormitory.

Space had been cleared on both sides of it, opposite the nuns' cells at the back. The pot was much too big for one burner. It covered both burners at once, and even a little more.

Down the middle of the stove and its two burners, the construction was secure enough. But along the other axis, it was a different matter altogether: more than half the pot tipped dangerously toward the front or back of the stove.

Talk about something being balanced precariously! Especially when there were fifty children in the dormitory.

Going to bed or getting up. Running in all directions, even though we weren't allowed to. Running to the bathroom, to get something to drink, to wash, to brush our teeth. In short, it was chaotic.

The very floor would shake. Fifty children can get even a concrete floor to shake!

In other words, whenever the floor shook, we could see the huge pot rocking back and forth. I'm not exaggerating when I say we could see it rocking.

Back and forth.

There was no danger of it spilling over the sides of the vanity: that was the stable axis, in line with the stove's burners. And the towel rack behind it would probably have put up enough resistance.

But toward the front, it was a worrying sight.

What would happen if the pot lurched forward? The question had been eating away at me ever since I saw the set-up.

I had seen the pot tip over a hundred times in my head.

One hundred times I had imagined the brown mixture come pouring out of the pot

— I reckoned the mixture had to be the same colour as the steam it gave off. One hundred times I had shuddered at the thought.

Which is why I always kept a calm, respectful distance between myself and the devil's cauldron. Not understanding why many of the other children appeared oblivious to the danger, coming within inches of the vanity as they ran past, walked backwards, pushed each other.

What was bound to happen finally happened.

But first, for the rest to make sense, everything has to be put in context.

The refectory was scrubbed from top to bottom once a week. The floor was mopped at night, after our usual bedtime.

On those nights, only half the children went to bed. The other twenty-five—we took turns—would spend an hour cleaning the refectory.

We pushed the tables and benches to one side. The children would then stand in line and get down on their knees to scrub, each holding their own brush.

We scrubbed, scrubbed, scrubbed, then mopped the floor. We shuffled back like that, until half the refectory had been cleaned.

We pushed the tables and benches back onto the clean side. We washed the other half. We pushed the tables and benches back to where they belonged. Then we went to bed.

That is what the other children did. Things weren't the same for me because of my special status.

I acted as an assistant to the nuns, like in the classroom.

And you wouldn't catch the nuns' assistant down on his hands and knees scrubbing a floor. Oh no, not on your life!

The assistant stood with the nuns, waiting to be asked to do this or that.

Perhaps they needed more floor mops, perhaps the water needed changing, or a brush had to be replaced. That night it was:

— Richard, go get the floor soap.

— Where is the floor soap, Mother?

— In the closet at the bottom of the vanity in the dormitory.

— You mean the small desk underneath the big pot in the middle of the dormitory?

— Yes, in the closet space at the bottom of that desk. Do not turn on the lights and do not make a sound or you will wake the children who are asleep.

Scared to death, I walked toward what I sensed was my fate. I walked up to the gates of hell, crouched down, and grabbed hold of the porcelain knob to open the door.

I pulled: nothing happened.

I pulled harder: still nothing. The door was locked, I decided.

I went back to the nun.

— It can't be—it doesn't have a lock!

— But I pulled really hard and the door didn't open.

— Richard, stop acting like a child. Just go get the floor soap, would you?

The nun was right: there was no lock.

It was the closing mechanism that made the vanity door hard to open. A metal rod with a ball on the end was attached to the inside of the door. There was a metal clip on the inside of the vanity. When you opened the door, both parts of the clip opened too and freed the metal ball.

In the other direction, the ball first forced the clip to open, then the clip closed over the metal rod: the door was closed.

You no doubt recognize a fixture that can still be found on most antiques and old kitchen closet doors today. You can't apply gradual pressure to open them. You have to pull sharply on the knob or handle. You close them sharply too.

Back to the door at the gates of hell.

First I gave gradual pressure a try. No luck: the door didn't budge an inch.

Then I knew what I had to do: open the doors with a sharp tug. But wouldn't that risk bringing the cooking pot crashing down? Especially since it could only fall forward, right on top of me.

I looked at the options available to me. I turned away from the vanity, ready to start the 100-metre dash.

My right hand behind my back, I grabbed hold of the knob. I would give it a sharp pull and start running at the same time. If nothing happened, I would be guilty only of being too careful. If the pot fell, I would be out of harm's reach.

Wasn't that a great plan?

Its only flaw was that it didn't work.

I crouched down, ready to break into a sprint. My right hand behind my back, I grabbed the knob.

One, two, three: go! I gave it a tug and took off. My right foot, the foot I was planning to explode off, slipped on the floor and I fell flat on my face.

It's amazing how time ground to a halt, everything that had time to come into my head. Flat on my face at the foot of the vanity, I told myself that if I was out of luck the pot had already begun to fall toward me.

I flung myself onto my back. And I saw it. In the pale glow of the night lights, I saw it.

I saw the pot already halfway down. I saw the strange liquid spilling out of it. Next came the pain. Indescribable pain.

The nun had told me not to make any noise so as not to wake up the children.

But I made such a racket! I picked myself up, roaring with all my strength. Out of the dormitory and into the central hallway.

I cried and I howled, jumping up and down on the spot.

What happened next might be hard to believe, but I swear it's the truth.

The nuns took me to the bathroom. They sprayed me with cold water and washed me. I needed a good wash since who knows what had been boiling in the pot. By this stage, I was passive and silent.

I must have fainted since the next second I was lying in my bed. Wrapped up so tightly in the covers that I couldn't move at all.

With all the lights on, it was as bright as daylight. Space had been cleared around my bed. My forty-nine comrades were on their knees in a circle, and one nun said:

— Pray for Richard who has just had a serious accident.

— Hail Mary, full of grace, the children chorused.

I prayed with them.

There was no arguing with Mother Superior. If she told you to pray, you prayed.

The praying went on for a while. Until around midnight, I'd say. Until the orphanage chaplain, Abbot Larouche, came back from a parish somewhere in the diocese.

Apparently I hadn't woken up only my floor. The chaplain found the whole orphanage in an uproar.

The nuns must have come up with some convoluted excuse or other. I suppose they must have felt guilty.

Guilty of what? I'll leave that up to you.

What I do know is that I saw the chaplain appear out of nowhere.

Rushing through the crowd, he took me in his arms. He ran through the orphanage and out to his car. He set me down on the back seat. And drove straight to the emergency room at the hospital in Chicoutimi.

What happened next is rather hazy.

Days followed nights, I imagine. I was covered from head to toe in bandages. Third-degree burns over half my body, second-degree burns everywhere else.

Later they told me it had been a close call, I was lucky to still be alive.

At the beginning, whenever they changed my bandages I couldn't feel a thing. It was almost as though they were doing it to someone else.

But later, when I was back to my usual self and my wounds had started to heal, I dreaded having to get my bandages changed almost every day.

The pain was on top of a fear of scarring: would I be disfigured for life?

Phew! My face and hands had only second-degree burns, which I was assured—and which I was later able to prove for myself—would leave no trace.

As for the rest of my body, they explained the skin that developed as I grew older would be perfectly normal. Between the age of seven and fifteen I was able to follow the progress of my scars as they gradually retreated.

In fact, they never did get any smaller. I was the one that grew.

All that remains is for me to tell you how my father reacted. At least, how people told me he reacted.

And what people continued to say for years thereafter, proudly, throughout the family.

In 1962 when all of this happened, my father was working on the construction site at Manic 5, the hydroelectric dam that is still the pride of Quebec today. Especially anyone who helped build it.

You should have heard my father for the rest of his life—the way he told it, he had built the whole thing himself!

At any rate, word reached my father at the Manic-5 site.

— Hurry, Monsieur Bergeron. One of your sons is dying in the Chicoutimi Hospital.

My father was there in a flash.

He must have taken the time to ask what was going on, though. Because the first visit he made wasn't to the hospital, but to the orphanage.

Imagine the scene. My father in the entrance hall. The nuns bowing and fawning all over him.

— Monsieur Bergeron, how dreadful! What a tragedy!

— That's enough, ladies. May I speak with Mother Superior?

Mother Superior was tiny, barely five feet tall, no doubt less than a hundred pounds. She rushed over like a little mouse, all aflutter, looking suitably shaken, which was only right and proper, of course, when meeting the father of the poor child that had just been burned from head to toe.

— Monsieur Bergeron—

She didn't get another word out.

My father had already punched her right in the face. She collapsed to the floor. A broken jaw and a concussion, they told me later. Which meant Mother Superior ended up in the hospital too, along with me.

They also said the whole thing was settled before it ever got to court: you don't sue us for burning your son and we won't sue you for flattening Mother Superior.

It sounds plausible enough because my father never heard another word about his unexpected visit to the orphanage.

It was only after that that my father apparently came to my bedside.

I say "apparently" because I didn't notice a thing. In fact, I can't remember anything at all about my first days in the hospital. Or maybe even my first weeks there.

I have two children of my own. A boy and a girl.

Their seventh birthdays were both very important to me.

They were so small, so beautiful when they were seven. So carefree and fragile, too, as children should be.

And both times I said to myself,

— Did I really go through all that at their age?

Today as I write these lines I can hardly believe it. I'm almost glad to still have the scars. To never forget.

To know it wasn't all a dream.

CONVALESCENCE

I must have spent something like three months in the hospital.

On the fortieth day—I know it was the fortieth because the adults wrote it down and told me later—I decided to get out of bed. But I don't need anyone to remind what had happened then.

Bang! I landed on the floor. The end of the world!

— I'll never walk again, just like Maman! I cried.

The nurses came running.

— Don't worry, Richard. You'll be up and running as much as you like. You just need us to help you.

The nurses were right. I walked, ran, and jumped so much that my last month in the hospital was like one long party.

Apart from when my bandages had to be changed, of course.

On the children's floor of a huge hospital, there is no shortage of children! Most arrive in a terrible mess, but in no time at all—as was the case for me—they're up for all kinds of games.

Some leave, others come in. The turnover was so high that I ended up teaching the others how to play since I'd been there so long.

The best game of all was also the simplest: jumping up and down on the beds. The nurses caught me and the other boys at it ten times. Once in so-and-so's bedroom, then someone else's.

They decided they had had enough of me wreaking havoc in their hospital. I was sent somewhere else to convalesce.

My convalescence was spent at my grandmother's. Two months of bliss.

You have had enough clues by now to have guessed there was something special between me and my grandmother. After those two months, our bond would last forever.

Was she a better grandmother than all the rest? I don't think so. I can tell you that when she had someone in her sights then he had better look out!

Her husband, my grandfather, for example. He made the mistake of cheating on her, more than once, on business trips to Quebec City and Montreal.

He was really something, Médéric Tibé Bergeron. The number one wood supplier to the paper mills in all of the Lac-Saint-Jean area.

He employed up to three hundred lumberjacks at once, split into four or five camps, in the middle of Parc des Laurentides and wherever else the paper companies had acquired logging rights from the government.

He also owned one of the nicest farms in Hébertville-Station, with up to one hundred draft horses.

You should have seen the looks on the faces of the old men in Saint-Cœur-de-Marie, L'Ascension, Métabetchouan, and any other village you care to name around the lake when they heard I was Tibé Bergeron's grandson. They had all worked for him. They couldn't stop talking about him.

Because times had been hard in the bush camps of the 1930s and '40s. And they didn't come much tougher than Tibé.

He had been hard on his men and his horses.

The men of L'Ascension would tell how six of them had been thrown outside in their underwear—through a camp window—because they refused to go and cut trees when it was minus forty-five.

And having seen these men two or three decades later, I can swear that real lumberjacks had been thrown out the window. The men who told me these stories weren't bitter, just full of admiration for my grandfather.

Others told me how a horse had been killed, stuck in deep snow and not able to move forward with its heavy load of logs.

— A horse that can't do its job deserves to die!

It was killed on the spot, flogged to death by Tibé Bergeron with the chains he used to fasten the logs.

With fifty horrified men looking on.

I should point out that I'm not at all sure either of these stories is true. Does a myth even need to be?

At any rate, Tibé met his Waterloo in the shape of his own wife when she found out he had been cheating on her.

She took her revenge all right, especially after the heart attack that left him half-paralyzed.

I was on my grandmother's side. I would annoy my grandfather however I could. By changing the channel when he was watching TV, by knocking against the back of his rocking chair, or by stealing his fork when we were eating.

Grand-papa would get worked up and insult me as best his laborious speech would allow. Grand-maman wasn't long in responding:

— Shut up, you old fool!

Not nice, not nice at all.

With some people, affinity comes naturally. I'd go as far as to say it's an animal instinct.

I may have been calculating with the nuns and plenty of others, but with Grand-maman I let myself go.

Give and take is nonetheless at the heart of all human relations. Love and respect and you will be loved and respected. Give and you will receive. How many people ruin their lives because they never understand these basic truths?

When I was a teenager, for as long as Grand-maman lived in her home in Alma, I went to see her every day.

We played cards, I went shopping for her, we watched television. When she moved into the home in Saint-Cœur-de-Marie, I had to make do with seeing her just once a week. Out there and home again on the bus every Saturday without fail.

My friends would laugh:

— Richard can't come Saturday afternoons. He's off to visit grandma!

— Screw you!

Once I started university in Montreal, it fell back to a phone call a week and five or six visits a year. Right up to end.

It was thanks to this providential convalescence that the bond was forever forged. Two months of quiet family life. Just Grand-maman, Grand-papa, me, and a boarder.

And I should point out that I wasn't pestering Grand-papa yet. That would have made me a real monster at seven. I didn't start until later. With my grandmother's unspoken approval.

Since I had missed over half the school year, the nuns were thinking about holding me back a year.

When Grand-maman got wind of that she flew into a rage:

— Give me his books and we'll soon see if he passes his year or not!

At the start of June, I went back to the orphanage. Grand-maman would have liked to keep me. But it wouldn't have been fair to my brothers. She explained it all to me; I understood.

Those two months of convalescence meant such a lot.

They made our relationship even stronger. Our relationship developed over time—over forty years, when you think about it. It's enough to make you wonder if I didn't scald myself on purpose.

Sometimes I'm not entirely sure.

WHAT
HAPPENED
NEXT

It was hard on my father knowing we were at the orphanage.

It humiliated him, and appeared to be proof he couldn't live up to his responsibilities. To take us back, first he would have to stop running off to far-flung construction sites.

The unbelievable number of construction sites in Montreal in preparation for Expo 67 gave him the chance to settle there. He also needed a wife, a housewife, someone to look after five children age six to ten.

Don't even think about my mother. She was out of the game for good.

He had found a replacement. I won't mention her name. You'll see why in a minute or two.

We were told the big news:

— The Bergerons, you are leaving the orphanage. You are going to live with your father in Montreal. You are so lucky!

And so we left for Montreal.

Seven of us in the car. My father, this woman, and what we'll still call the baby up front. The four eldest piled in on top of each other on the back seat.

What we didn't know was that we were leaving for Montreal in early January only to come back to Lac-Saint-Jean by the end of May.

My father was on edge. He snapped at the woman. He swore. He put whole sentences together using only swear words. Accompanied by a few harsh words for the feminine condition.

Things got louder as the case of beer emptied. To the point where he cuffed her around the head. In the back seat, we were worried sick. What had we gotten ourselves into? I must have thought.

Not to mention that we didn't even know this man all that well.

After what seemed an eternity, we arrived in Montreal.

Rue LaSalle, just down from Ontario, in the Maisonneuve district.

A two-bedroom apartment for seven people. The five children in the same bedroom. We were used to it. And five is still less than fifty!

We were still exploring the apartment when my father found another reason to shout and swear at the woman.

She made the mistake of answering back.

The five of us hid in the bedroom, the door slightly ajar, and missed nothing of the scene that followed.

My father took a run-up and punched the woman in the face. She collapsed against the refrigerator, unconscious.

My father sat down at the kitchen table and opened another bottle of beer. He saw we were watching and shouted over:

— Go to bed, you little bastards!

We were in bed in two seconds flat.

The woman came back round when my father was asleep. She found her own way to the hospital. Don't ask me how.

A broken jaw and concussion. Just like Mother Superior. She said she fell down the stairs. That's what they all said back then.

And when they were asked why they covered up for their husbands, they said:

— Because I love him!

The tone was set for the rest of our stay in Montreal. It would be pretty much more of the same.

Life in the apartment was sheer madness.

After work my father would stop at the tavern for several hours. The woman did her best to keep us under control, making sure we ate. And my father would invariably come home to find the apartment turned upside down, with five hyper children at ten o'clock at night.

It was time to show some authority.

He would take off his belt and beat us once or twice at random. He was drunk so he didn't worry how hard.

It didn't feel the same as when the nuns beat us. When he saw us writhing in pain and bawling our eyes out, he would be overcome by remorse:

— OK, OK, stop your crying. I'll come play with you.

And there he was, our father clambering up on top of a desk, jumping onto the nearest bed. He weighed over two hundred pounds; the bed exploded. With enough noise to wake the dead.

We laughed and laughed! When suddenly the doorbell rang.

It was the police again, come to tell us to keep the noise down. The neighbours ended up getting us thrown out.

We went through three different apartments in barely five months.

Children our age went to school. In theory, at least.

We went a few times to the local school where our father had signed us up. It was a five-minute walk away: that wasn't the problem.

The other children were the problem.

Dyed-in-the-wool Montreal kids in a working-class neighbourhood that had four pubs on every corner took great delight in beating up the "country bumpkins from Lac-Saint-Jean."

We were a welcome distraction for them. In the schoolyard, during recess, on the way to school, before and after class—or even, for the boldest—during class as soon as the teacher had his back turned.

Fresh out of the orphanage, we didn't know how to defend ourselves. And if we had, that would probably only have made things worse. We were outnumbered, plain and simple.

And so for the day or two we went to school, we came home in a real mess, our faces bruised, our clothes torn.

— Stop going. It's no big deal, my father concluded.

How did he manage it with the school board? God only knows.

This rowdy bohemian lifestyle nevertheless had its fair share of good times.

Like the time we went sliding where the Olympic Stadium stands today.

When Papa was home, sober, and made us his "super pancakes."

When he took us out for a drive in the car.

When we watched the afternoon movies on Channel 10.

It wasn't at all like the orphanage!

My father wasn't a bad man. He just had a lot of weight on his shoulders. And years of living alone and mulling things over in his head had led to some very bad habits. Starting with drinking.

He eventually faced facts.

But there was no way he was sending us back to the orphanage. Especially since times were changing and there was talk of shutting down the orphanage in Chicoutimi.

The new formula was social services: placing children with families. But who would ever want to take a child who had already grown up and only receive a measly monthly cheque in return?

Well farmers always need extra hands. And so off to farms we went.

As soon as we were back in Alma, I took Grand-maman to one side and asked if I could stay with her. She said yes, but only for two years.

Two years is a lifetime when you've not yet turned ten.

Two of the youngest left for farms right away. The youngest was first taken in by a family—a child of six is still cute—before ending up on a farm too.

The eldest and I lived for two years with our grandmother, as promised, before heading to farms of our own.

I know you're going to say I'm repeating myself, but they really were two years of bliss.

Two years that started with Grand-maman beside herself with anger when she found out the principal of L'École Saint-Joseph—we called him Ti-Jet—was refusing to let me take the end of year exams. For reasons you can imagine.

One meeting was enough for Ti-Jet to change his mind. And I finished top of the class.

As was only right and proper!

❖

What happened next? Life. Life happened next. Just life.

A People's History of Quebec
Jacques Lacoursière & Robin Philpot

An Independent Quebec
The past, the present and the future
Jacques Parizeau, former Premier of Quebec

Trudeau's Darkest Hour
War Measures in Time of Peace, October 1970
Edited by Guy Bouthillier & Édouard Cloutier

The Question of Separatism
Quebec and the Struggle over Sovereignty
Jane Jacobs

The Riot that Never Was
The military shooting of three Montrealers in 1832
and the official cover-up
James Jackson

Soldiers for Sale
German "Mercenaries" with the British in Canada during
the American Revolution 1776-83
Jean Pierre Wilhelmy

The First Jews in North America 1760-1860
The Extraordinary Story of the Hart Family
Denis Vaugeois (translated by Käthe Roth)

America's Gift
What the World Owes to the Americas
and Their First Inhabitants
Käthe Roth and Denis Vaugeois

Going Too Far
Essays About America's Nervous Breakdown
Ishmael Reed

Slouching Towards Sirte
NATO's War on Libya and Africa
Maximilian Forte (October 2012)